THE
DIRIGIBLE
CHRONICLES

zerby pux

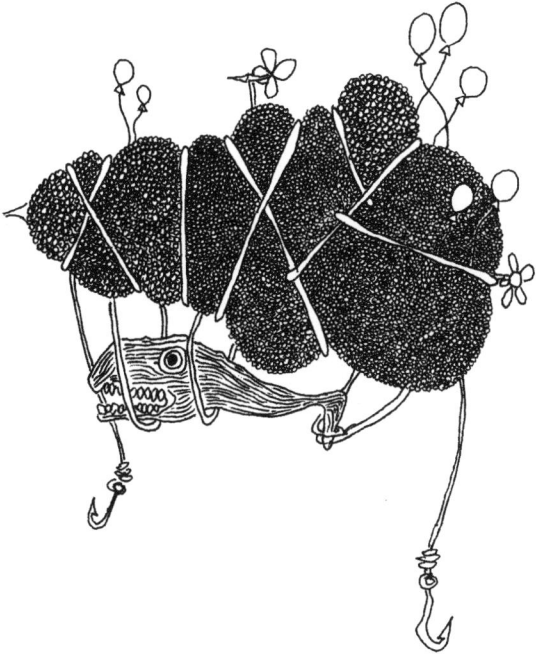

The Dirigible Chronicles

To all those who've wanted to
throw their phone in the ocean,
Cheers.

(And Bobbie Alexander,
who knows a thing or two
and has a laugh along the way).

MERCY

Where will it splinter,
or where will it stall,
begging of gravity
to surrender it all.

The pompous raindrop
has so far to fall.

DIRIGIBLE THIS

The stars are bright
on this desolate flight.

A rainbow of color
tinting the duller
seas below.

MELLIFONT ABBEY

Creeping in the
shadow stream,
jumping through
the murk,

the ruins all
around us,
beware the soul of
church.

In its day
was splendor
now it's just
a waste.

The pilgrims come
a' knocking
but not for
salvation's sake.

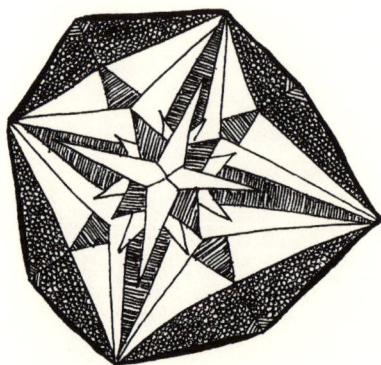

MERE SAVAGES

Reckless wanderers
obey the compass
with cold disdain.

In the end
the world is atoms
with ion buzzing force.

No amount of meddling
can stop the course
as we hurtle past the light.

SELDOM OAK

Hollow bodies
yearn for more,
walking empty
'cross the moor.

The lonely forest
has a tree,
growing sadly
bent on knee.

Chills go shallow
down the line,
winter's coming
one last time.

MOUNT DESERT ISLAND

Into autumn
time carries me,
thirty year
and counting.

I join a rock
in solitude
with stubborn
spindle tree.

The granite waits
with patience,
until he
touches sea.

How long will eons
wither him
until he
rests with me.

THE HALLOWED SON

The sun
rose this morning,
riddled in fear.

The planets
looked moody,
brooding quite clear.

The coldness,
the empty,
the darkness,
the dear,

why must he burn,
forever hot sphere.

Nothing, no nothing
could come to him near.

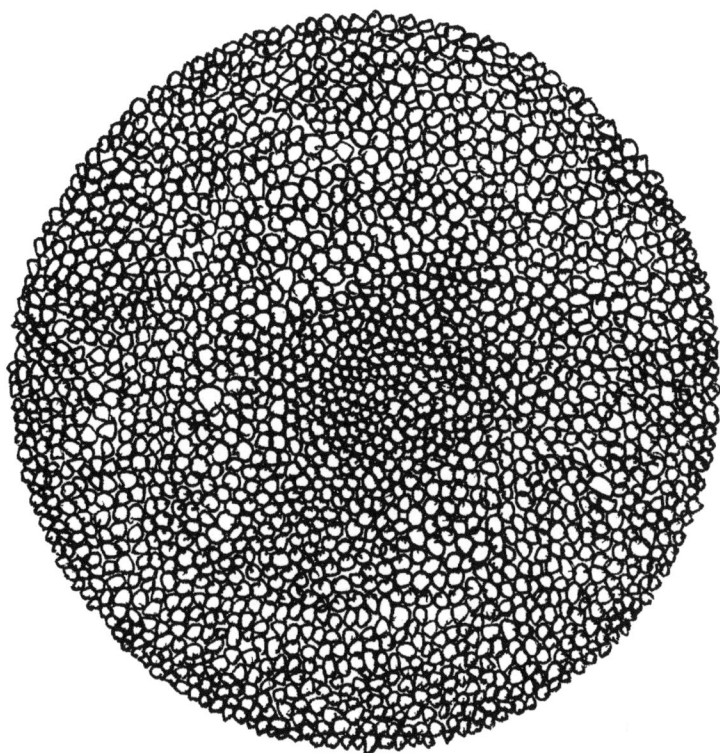

MIDNIGHT SOUR

Into light,
out of darkness,
once dwelt these feet
in sad defeat.

UNFOUND

Sifting through
the barrow downs
and the dunes
beneath the mountain,

the rain forgets
to wash away
the spectre
of the night.

A spark of yellow
marks a grave
lost unto the ages.

Sleeping souls
do wander blind
in the mountain,
mountain grind.

RESTLESS IN SEPTEMBER

I do not want
this life to end,
nor do I wish it
to continue.

The piano moans
an icy tone
and humbles
at the rest note.

How dare the silence
never tremble
with weakened knees
of anxious trouble.

The compass follows
feet and toes
no matter where
the needle shows.

SHEPHERD WEAK

Onward goes
the ever death,
eating days
of halting breath.

Taught to fight
for nails and teeth,
grubbing for
the honey.

What halts the hope
of eternal sheep
but dreaming of
a thousand sleep.

He will call,
the Shepherd Weak,
to take you down
with those you seek.

SHIPWRECK CHOWDER

The fog has settled
with blinding grace,
and left this
world befuddled.

WET SOCKS, WARM FEET

Wading from the
salt salt sea
five long months
forsaken.

Kingdoms come
and kingdoms fray,
I've gone to search
beyond the bay.

12.1437 | 77.1090

A boy waits patient
for inspiration,
beneath the
looming sunset.

Time will pause
as hands stop still,
nestled neatly
in hazy thrill.

MY UNBORN CHILD

I've marched up mountains
of earthly realms
and bathed amongst
the clouds.

Suns will split
with meager light
through autumn's
golden height.

Shattered cargo
of molten dreams,
of love and
children wild.

The barrow ghosts
laugh and ponder,
why never were
they made?

HOPEWELL GIANT

Hopewell pigeons
flock of bats
hidden in the tunnel.

Out of darkness
they warble flap
watching tides in bay.

The heads of giants
wrought of stone
watch the human spout.

Some day he'll travel
to water brave,
headless and devout.

GLOBAL MOONS

Hardened secrets
held and hewn,
passing whispers,
papers strewn.

Shadow walk
the caging surf
with memory faded
beyond this earth.

Write the wrong
to cure the moon
as tides begin
to wrinkle prune.

SACRED THREE

The sacred three
once spoken
cannot be forgot.

It whistles off the canyons
and trickles through the swamp.

It eats the soul
until it rots,
or flowers vastly,
long and hot.

The sacred three
were woken,
the sacred three
were spoken,

and now I
cannot stop.

APPENDIX

A vestigial heart
still knows to beat,
but only once
a sparing minute.

SAINT MALO STUMBLE

The walls have tumbled down
after standing through the ages.
The rats will nibble before they drown
and demand their scummy wages.

The crashing ocean,
the palsied leaf,
the waxing gibbis,
the withered thief.

All have aimed
to conquer stone,
but king stands
cunning all alone.

The rats have entered
your domain
and once they've started
your life's in vain.

A GROUND AXE

Ground the axe
into the field
and coax the
furrowed lot.

A boulder thrown
is long forgot
as the glacier
fills the bay.

Thrones will quiver
as iron breaks
and shoots of green
will overtake.

SILENCE IN THE MIST

One tree is dead
among the millions
but a regal
sight it be.

These Kings will rise
and fall with dread,
a copper moon emerging,
dangling overhead.

The wind has battered
and beaten grey
the roots once
green and fed.

These gritty bluffs
will shroud a land
as the needles
curl and fall.

SHEEP

The sheep
control the shepherd,
the nature
rules the man.

The thought of death
will steal the fear
as lightning
bows to man.

Time leaks by
but the wrist
controls the watch.

Cogs will discontinue
but the world
will never stop.

Power lies in pieces
'til sheep bare
their wooly wrath.

Only then will
the gladful shepherd
book a last vacation,
and pick a different flock.

IT WILL END IN CHAOS,
JUST AS THE PAGAN SAID

He bowed on knees
and bled on altar
and listened
to an unforgiving god.
(frown)

'What's done is done
and cannot be undone'.

'You've lived a life
but with a knife
you bleed upon my altar'.

'The tails of sacrifice
fly 'twix your crooked
parchment lips'.

'What's done is done
and cannot be undone
by mere gods
nor savage mortal'.

'All that's left
is a resting knee
and whispered
words of sorrow
careening down
an empty. (tunnel)'.

LIGHTYEAR

A fornicating god
has lost his way
once more.

The people lost
his mantle
as the ships
began to soar.

No tired resignation
can still his inner force.
Thus the sea is humid and
thick with (c)old discourse.

OPENING OVERTURE

triple beat
times seven
21 dead
rest notes
hollow in my
throat

where'd the
lyric go
pasted on
a goat

it's an
acapella
apocalypse
silence
in
my
ear

HAIKU

in the dead of night
the world cradled in deep sleep,
rage at a canvas.

KINGS & PRAWNS

The power brays of pleasantries,
  the pigeons clucking fool.

I'm sure it's in the riddle
  this tower jabbing tool?

Sandwiched in the velvet cushion
  this fox-wood fiddle rules.

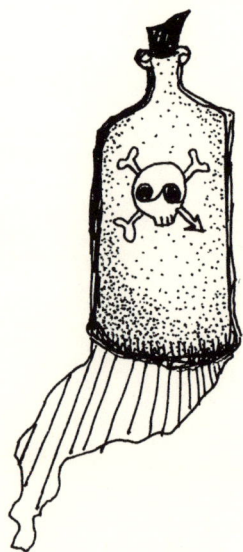

CREEP DECAY

Pick your poison
or none at all
'cause in the end
they'll all trip fall.

And Kings will
bend on knee
and beg to just go free.

DIRGE (FUNERAL HYMN)

sweet potato pancake
pocket kicks a beat
twenty times a
tire.

time to retire.

INK BLOT

May you dream of
trains of thought
more worthy
than ink blot.

ARM PIT PUNCH

Inside the
skeleton is
the lock to
the worldly
bilch storm.
arm pit
lasers will
erase Erasmus.

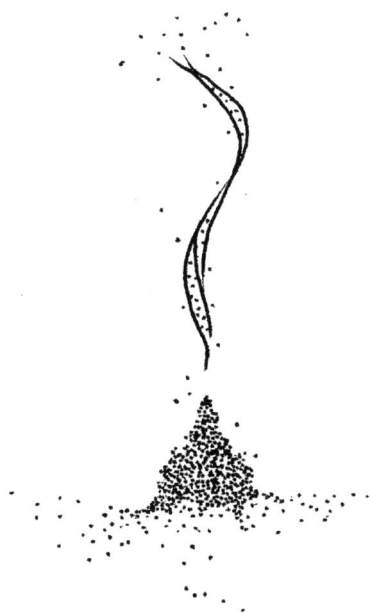

PARTY OF ONE

Dress shoes and power tools
dancing through the night.

The sawdust settles
under step, as the jig
makes merry music.

Tap the heels
as sparks ignite
singeing age old matter.

CIVILIZED ROT

So daring,
so darling,
so darting,
so daft.

Excuse this misuse
but damn the arsonist,
the arson,
the victim, the fire.

Vanquish the crooked,
the wicked, the lot.

Newscaster rates
mass Murder
of monkeys
as the sociable recluse
longs for parties of one.

SWAMP EDDY STRANGER

Life's in danger
ain't no stranger
bad enough to skill
a billet off a hill,

a little bully
can only buck
a trendy
Saint Nickel.

Sit atop an
atom bomb
snorkel in a
sewer swamp,

but don't sit scared
upon a sacred thought,
these dreams are forged
but never bought.

DIETICIAN'S DETRIMENT

Eat the cannibal
to teach a lasting lesson.

Throw in spices
to leg him on the spit.
Toast it,
roast it,
falling from the bone.

Maybe it'll taste of human,
or McDonald's and
stale old beer,
that's the biggest fear.

JUICE

Ear wax tastes of
coroner juice and
other things once dry.

RUBBERNECK SALOON

Spittle spittoon
after
crab Rangoon,
killer
red dragoon.

EL DORADO FIREFLY

If El Dorado
is a place
I'd be loathe
to go and visit.

It sounds like
Vegas strippers
miraging in a desert,
pasted on a bill-boar.

The cannibal eats
a mistress
and thus
I digress
to whittled words
of golding rust.

UNRIGHT BUDDHA

Rising with the tide
well spent,
diving in the
words soft sent.

My heart is filled
with rage he said,
at the second
double crossing.

This world will
ever be
but discontent.

KINETIC MAYHEM

The sand clock
hoards the fallen grain,

wished those praying
of a modest rain.

A forest of fires
will bring to the brink,

and ink dries fierce
the more it thinks.

ANALOGUE DAY DREAM

Dog
is
med
said Nietzsche
in catacombs
unfed.

Medicine will cure us
of everything I've said.

Sit and listen
to the vision
and fill the clog
with lead.

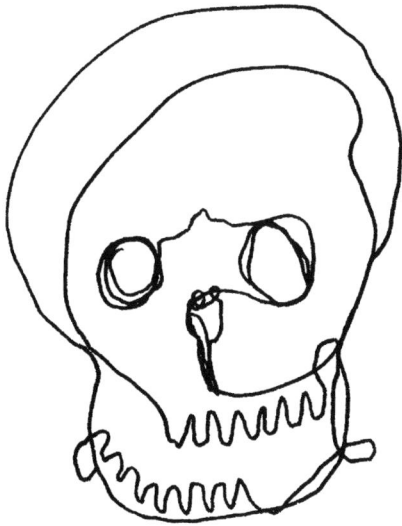

FAIRFUS OF BABYLON

I regret to say the
Fairfus of Babylon
shoots films in the
wee hours of the morn.

Have fun refereeing
small scale librarians
booking shelves
betwixt A-Zed.

SUBMARINE

Does a cell phone
skip of stone
as it skims along
the ocean.

You'll get one toss
of titan loss,
as it sinks
beneath the surface.

HUMANITY

The burden weighs heavy
as the air will not breathe.

Cornered and craven
these dreams come unfree.

Is strength measured
in patience or pain,

a rock and an ocean
make perilous grain.

This land has endured,
sober stars can attest,

lofty and weightless,
aloof to man's (my) quest.

ELDEST STONE

Have you found
the lichen speech
hard and cold
to read.

Lichens are
a hardy lot
found on stones
unfriendly.

ROAD ROBINSON

I walk a hundred
mile with no shoe.

I search this world
for what is true.

What inspires such a man
but obsession scorching through.

The foot will sound
upon the ground
'til toes are spent
and truth is found.

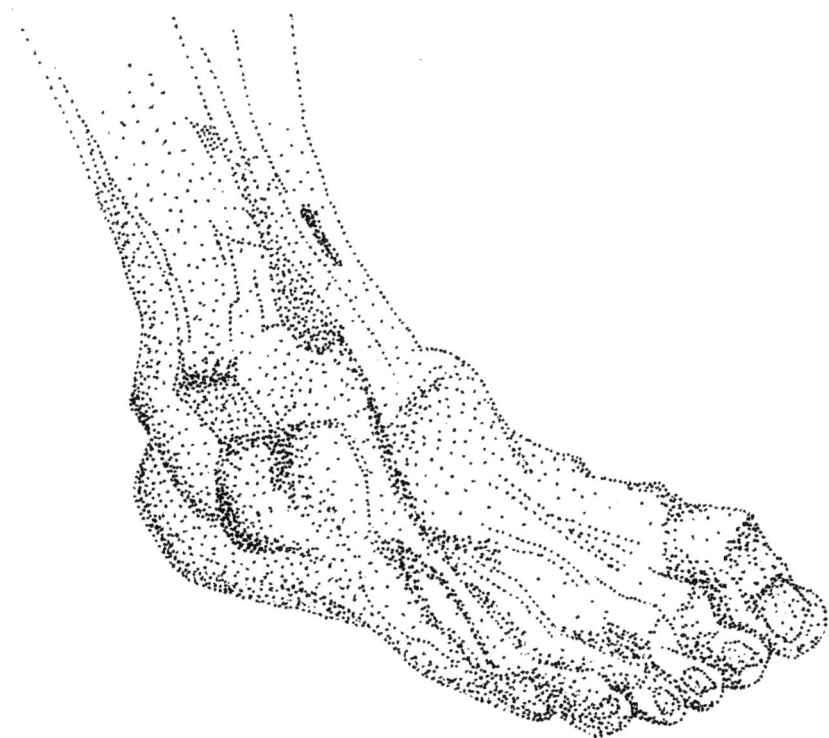

NOVA CORE GALORE

Far into the sky I crept,
seeking answers
unbeswept.

Thoughtful minds
don't always speak,
passive listeners
tonight do seek.

The claxon pales
to quickened beat
of bleakened worries
(thr)obselete.

Golden skies
of ruined time
promised bright,
this final climb.

LOYALTY LOST

I am not free
like you and me,
shackled at the start.

This road is traveled
by the dreamer
full of bridges crossed.

I had a way
in which I walked
never calculating cost.

These tolls are heavy on a hearth
that warms only for those
who have been lost.

FOREIGN WEALTH

The loneliness
of riches
is discovered
on the lake.

Told and barren
is the place
where devils
go to lace.

Private beaches
belie the quest
searching ever
for lively zest.

Nomads wander
and wonder less,
which riches
serve them best.

DECADENT DRUDGERY

The wandering prophet
simply sees
more than he can know.

The time of rancid dinners
was never nearly lost.

Stone church soup
is filled with rocks
and matter made of atoms.

No work but what
a bonus alley day.

The journey beckons
with its secret promise,
dreams the lonesome prophet.

DEER BONE STEW

Boiling bucket (bouquet) of bones
burping brothy bubbles.

Nostril lingers like a tomb
this dinner smells of doom.

GHOST KNIGHT

The plunge was swollen,
the knife decayed,
as the shining helmet
touched with grey.

The Ghost Knight knows
of only way,
even if it be
the cruelest day.

A CLEARING IN THE FOREST

I will not fear
the death I live.

A sun filled grove
will take me in,
nature mended
and branches thin.

The glass will dirty,
the honey soak,
but I will rest
in sunny smoke.

The ancient hemlock,
bent and low
shelters pilgrims
though no one shows.

Bury me with
mem'ries dear
for some have lasted
while I'm here.

Wither through
the coming years
drinking salt
and waxing ears.

And when I lie
above my bed
peering down at
grey old head,

I'll fear not living
for I'll be dead.

NUCLEUS

Is there trouble understood,
brewing costly
as she could.

Darkened dreams
taste bittersweet
as the coffin
begins to steep.

In this saga
I never sleep,
and cold winds enter
this castle keep.

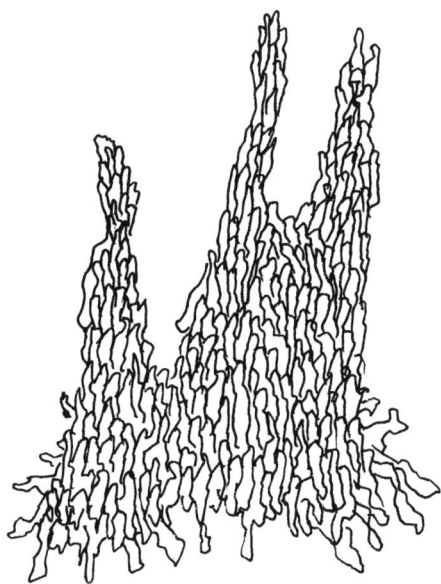

DUSTY GRANITE DEADSTONE

The rusted mind
graks and grinkles,
tick-aling a fancy
that just won't go away.

Tar will ooze
from bubbling bulbs
to singe the skin
in law blade splatter.

What happened to this
tarnished rage
that took an age to sow?

Rent a knee and pray
it'll never go away,
'til all that's left is rubble
at the bottom of my

dusty
granite
deadstone.

(T)RUMINATE

Heavy time will crush
the toasted bread rye.

This daily rush
is a turbulent lie,
as the sky turns bluer
with a lasting sigh.

Himmit,
and deeply truminate, why.

GOULASH

The melancholy page
seeps with stewing sentences.

Boiled kettles bubble and squeak
and creep of tea
made of lavender, sadness
and goulash.

DELUGE(IONAL)

What is the point
of muddied buckets
full of leaden paint?

Rats have scampered,
squirrels have fled,
but the mouse remains
are dead.

The cold salt screams
upon the wound
but a face won't
bat a flicker.

Earthly trouble,
the dwellers dark,
senses double
as it hits their mark.

SILVER DARK MASK

The most aristocratic loser
sits upon the lonely throne.

He moans to lofty music
and sings to polished stone.

There's nothing more pathetic
to the voyeur looking in,

but the king will find
his pleasure with naught but
paint and gin.

WHAT IS A GILOR?

Bull skull
vicar(ious) cigar
sharp rolls
galore.

What is a Gilor?

Rocket twisted
high cowboy socket
finger line
down spine

rib trickle
snarch.

The power lines flow
from horn to horn

and the femur dangles
from hip.

LOGICAL PSYCHO

Message in a
throttle
I'm gonna eat your
bottle.
Food for thought,
The Road.
Axe, meat, eat.

Blind the thrice
eye your meal
crown the Puma
into oblivion
goes the Lion
Prince of the
Baobab Lands
no more.

The logical psycho
longs for company
of Egrets
regrets the

shrink
who expounds
the Masters
foul play
into prison
the doctor rots
Ph.D
Pounding Human
Desire
in his white tooth
holes.

Message in a
throttle
the beat echoes off
the inner cranium
'til the Cows howl
at the moon and
keep the Wolves at
bay.

LUNCH

The edible termite
tastes of
wood chips
glue and rot.

TOASTY TOES

The sleepwalking centipede
roams the halls,
dodging puddling squalls.

Best foot leads
the beasty bug to bed
to rest a tired head.

SLEEP WRITING

The restless mind
walks the
fourth dimension,
a Phoenix in a cage.

The restless mind
has conversations
with piglets
and abnormations.

In the end the
fourth dimension
is a place of
barren plains,

where creatures
live off thinkly
thoughts of
futures from the past.

Old pink memories
blaze from ashes
wafting from the stage.

What did not happen
transpires here,
in the fourth dimension
of restless walking brains.

MOLTEN AMNESIA

My mind was molten,
hurt and bare,
my body flexed
in disrepair.

But now I know
that truth is cold
as water stains
the sink.

Blood is red,
this rage is dead
as you drift to sit
beside me.

KING OF MATTER

The holy mind
is filled with
blowing thistles.

A crow can fall
from the meteor sky,
a crown will stall
with a breathless lie.

The smirking horse
will run the course
but never wear a smile.

Defeat the coma
with swallows frail,
or drink the mud from
a rusted pail.

Do you wish to wear
this crown,
tarnished by the weather.

SHADOWS OF THE GLIMPSE

I walked into
another's mind
just to see if
I'd survive.

A master wades
amongst the failures
just to breathe
a former life.

Let me use
the granite gas mask
so I'll die a
little slower.

The key drops lower
to a whisper
as the truth begins
to settle.

I cannot fathom
the lonely of another
for my mind
would simple laughter
(falter).

A SILENT DEATH

The dying leaf
is beautiful
as it withers
on the tree.

Imagine if
a human
turned yellow,
red and free.

It tumbles toward
the frosted earth
and settles on
its course,

tossed forever
in the wind,
collecting with
his brothers.

The dying leaf is beautiful
as it rests
'neath winters
soundless sleep.

ANCIENT ONE

Bones will rustle
'neath the cairns,
with mem'ries
long forgot.

Leaves of autumn
wasted bare
as parchment
dried and spare.

No sons to weep,
nor daughters care
to pay the ancient ferry.

Who buries bones
of lonesome hermits,
but time and leaves
and rock.

DANSE MACABRE

This mind is not like yours,
it thrives on doom unmeasured.
Is it true about the tortured soul,
of crumbling starts and treason.

I stand on feet
made of anger, toes and bone.
They march the path
on grizzled pastures weak.

But in the end
I quiver in the dark
of mind and matter
and await a gruesome day.

Flowers bloom
from a tomb
made of concrete
and marbled rubble.

The gathering sways
as the skeleton prances
to a stony beat,
for The Grim will fast no longer.

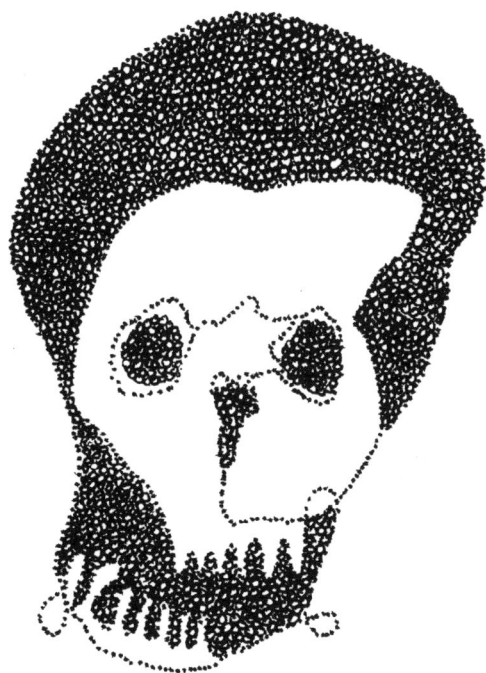

SUNSET SUDDEN

Lost in worlds
and heavy scree,
this weightless mountain
haunting.

I see the skies
that follow me
and brave
another step.

How did it end
with storms
and spite,
conquered by this dying light.

KRAKEN

The bitter kraken
tips a ship
and always dreams
of plunder.

RED & DEAD

Scratch the surface
to see a cloud
red with age
and sorrow.

Chiseled bone
can pick a tooth
to free you
of the marrow.

TRUTH

Truth can burn
an awful wage
through the
deepest pocket.

PYRE & GRIMSTONE

Fifteen fickle
fishbots
flopping on
a sidewalk.

Don't decide
to ditch
the water
before you
flip or flop.

GRINK

Late mid-day breakfast
is only oddly for
the otherly (m)eaters.

The grink knows not
the tastely wonder
of bubbular caviar.

Wild-eyed
inside a pocket watch,
late middle twilight.

A LAYERED SHELL

Child beggars eat
meals of kings
with fingers and a smile,

while the fashionable turtle
wears a helmet
to the festival of faces.

He thinks of sweet
dragonflies and
warm chocolate puddles.

Wear your boot
'til your toes grow thin
and remember where
your life's begin.

INEVITABLE NEANDERTHAL

The sinking stone
may try to swim
but the best he'll do is skip.

The perfect man
knows not what he wants
but precisely what he is.

KINGDOM OF (N)ONE

The penguin king
peers left and late,
searching for his mate.

Alas she's gone
for another date,
longing for a finer fate.

APPARITION BLUES

A world once left behind
will be difficult to find.

The time has gone,
the clock has settled,
the moon is shining,
the sun has nestled.

Eyes close to the
music swaying tree
and the dancing tempo of
love lost free.

PERMANENCE

The truth is
made of permanence
though time
can't last forever.

Mirrors bend
the truth in line,
casting shadows
on the season.

FREEDOM, FREEDOM

The stars need not fall
from the perilous sky,
shining and brilliant
before they die.

The darkness is looming
as I watch you cry,
power and choice
lost in a sigh.

If one word
could kindle a heart,
I beg freedom, freedom,
the promise from start.

VOYAGERS

Why do lovers
sit and stare
at the sunset
getting lower.

All need do is
keep on walking
to make it last forever.

ORCHARDS EATEN

Apples blossom
in the orchard
but are eaten
all the same.

Leave it peaceful
in the rain
for summer freezes
and winter drains.

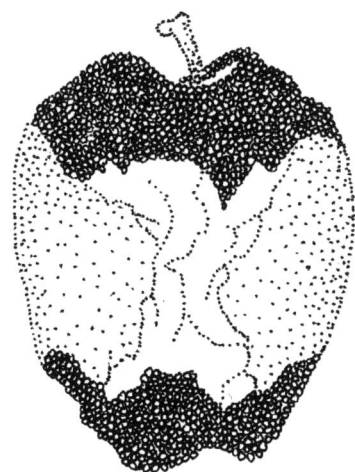

SWITCHER CANE

The forest fire
burns the truth,
the lies and
speckled matter.

Thus a mind
alights in flame,
no quarter left
for thee.

The purge is sudden,
hot and bright,
but leaves just
cold, cold sight.

DEVIL'S WAKE

Grief is guarded
in Scoundrel safe,
it breathes so softly
in Devil's wake.

The Road to nowhere
out the past,
litter strewn
it ends aghast.

King Tut mourned
for longer days,
wrapped in gold
we sing his praise.

Stars have fallen
in a chest
locked and borrowed
at Grief's behest.

COLD NIGHTS

The frozen earth,
the callous hand,
the steaming shovel
on the land.

The acres tumble
under foot,
winter's crunching,
ember soot.

The trees are wary
of the wind,
stripping naked
to the skin.

The silent owl
watches sound,
mouse hooves thrashing,
crashing down.

This simple soul
is buried
with empty
words unfound.

MAN MADE FOOLS

The kayak master
floats from shore
to drink the pagan thunder.

With blinding light
awash this night
and heave these heavens open.

DUST SETTLES DOWNWARD

At the hour of crickets
the earth will stop spinning
this dizzying dream.

Every rock will come joyous,
flowing and bare.

The extinction of humans,
no one will care.

The graves rot in ruin,
the dead cannot spare.

Bombs rust like diamonds,
oozing with mud
as I stare up the mountain,
drowning white flood.

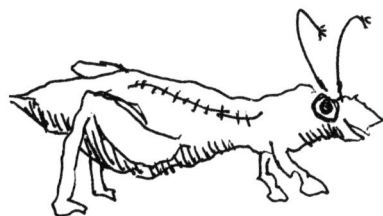

∞

The sun is always shining
above the dirty cloud.

It never sleeps
nor ever wavers,

its sentence
forever bound.

The masses take it granted,
this fact so obsolete.

What hollow world
this place would be

when darkness holds
the telling key.

VESUVIUS FALLING

Empty is the land,
our exit slow and sad.

Where once was left
a bone and sand,
now lingers
hardened man.

Lost is history's
awkward whisper,
of guns and lies
so grand.

We are not the ones
to stand,
and burn to ash
this sacred land.

RAINIER

Leaning trees
are toothpicks
in the mountain shadow.

Aged and green
with hallowed beards,
know nothing of their plight.

A thousand year
they've trusted,
the land, the sand, the right.

Grown and bred
and silent sight
the forest lives tonight.

Is it fate, or is it folly,
to worship gods
of latent might.

UGLY

The ugly raindrop
wraps itself
in the teeming
masses.

It lingers clear
in misted fear,
'til ocean worn
it crashes.

(T)Ruminate, 70
∞ , 112
12.1437 | 77.1090, 17

A Clearing in the Forest, 66
A Ground Axe, 25
A Layered Shell, 96
A Silent Death, 85
Analogue Day Dream, 51
Ancient One, 86
Apparition Blues, 99
Appendix, 22
Arm Pit Punch, 39

Civilized Rot, 42
Cold Nights, 107
Creep Decay, 36

Danse Macabre, 87
Decadent Drudgery, 62
Deer Bone Stew, 64
Deluge(ional), 72
Devil's Wake, 106
Dietician's Detriment, 45

Dirge (Funeral Hymn), 37
Dirigible This, 3
Dust Settles Downward, 109
Dusty Granite Deadstone, 69

El Dorado Firefly, 48
Eldest Stone, 56

Fairfus of Babylon, 53
Foreign Wealth, 61
Freedom, Freedom, 101

Ghost Knight, 65
Global Moons, 20
Goulash, 71
Grink, 95

Haiku, 33
Hallowed Son, 9
Hopewell Giant, 19
Humanity, 55

Inevitable Neanderthal, 97
Ink Blot, 38

It Will End In Chaos, Just as
    the Pagan Said, 29

Juice, 46

Kinetic Mayhem, 50
King of Matter, 81
Kingdom of (N)One, 98
Kings & Prawns, 34
Kraken, 90

Lightyear, 30
Logical Psycho, 76
Loyalty Lost, 60
Lunch, 77

Man Made Fools, 108
Mellifont Abbey, 4
Mercy, 2
Mere Savages, 6
Midnight Sour, 11
Molten Amnesia, 80
Mount Desert Island, 8
My Unborn Child, 18

Nova Core Galore, 59
Nucleus, 67

Opening Overture, 31
Orchards Eaten, 103

Party of One, 41
Permanence, 100
Pyre & Grimstone, 93

Rainier, 114
Red & Dead, 91
Restless in September, 13
Road Robinson, 57
Rubberneck Saloon, 47

Sacred Three, 21
Saint Malo Stumble, 24
Seldom Oak, 7
Shadows of the Glimpse, 84
Sheep, 28
Shepherd Weak, 14
Shipwreck Chowder, 15
Silence In the Mist, 26
Silver Dark Mask, 74
Sleep Writing, 79
Submarine, 54
Sunset Sudden, 89
Swamp Eddy Stranger, 44
Switcher Cane, 105

Toasty Toes, 78
Truth, 92

Ugly, 115
Unfound, 12
Unright Buddha, 49

Vesuvius Falling, 113
Voyagers, 102

Wet Socks, Warm Feet, 16
What is a Gilor?, 75

50749926R00076

Made in the USA
Middletown, DE
01 July 2019